M000073469

LARRY BURKETT

SOUND BUSINESS PRINCIPLES

MOODY PRESS
CHICAGO

© 1993 by
LARRY BURKETT

Scripture quotations, unless noted otherwise,
are taken from the *New American Standard
Bible*, © 1960, 1962, 1963, 1968, 1971, 1972,
1973, 1975, and 1977 by The Lockman Foun-
dation. Used by permission.

Portions of this booklet have been adapted
from Larry Burkett, *Using Your Money Wisely*
(Chicago: Moody, 1986), © 1985 by Christian
Financial Concepts; and from Larry Burkett,
Business by the Book (Thomas Nelson), ©
1990 by Larry Burkett.

*Edited by Adeline Griffith
Christian Financial Concepts*

ISBN: 0-8024-2613-1

1 3 5 7 9 10 8 6 4 2

Printed in the United States of America

About the Author

Larry Burkett is committed to teaching God's people His principles for managing money. Unfortunately, money management is one area often neglected by Christians, and it is a major cause of conflict and disruption in both business and family life.

For more than two decades Larry has counseled and taught God's principles for finance across the country. As president of Christian Financial Concepts, Larry has counseled, conducted seminars, and written numerous books on the subject of maintaining control of the budget. In addition he is heard on more than 1,000 radio outlets worldwide.

Sound Business
Principles

WHAT IS
CHRISTIAN BUSINESS?

O bviously there is no such thing as "Christian business." A business is a legal entity, such as a corporation, partnership, or proprietorship and, as such, has no spirit or soul. It may, however, reflect the values of the principal owners or managers. It is the reflection of these values that determines whether or not a business is labeled Christian or non-Christian.

In James 1:22 we are told to be "doers" of the Word. A business is the perfect environment for applying Christ's teachings and, if put in God's hands, can be used to demonstrate the truth of the gospel.

APPLYING GOD'S RULES

One of the best ways to determine whether a business is being

5

used to serve God is to look at the policies governing the day-to-day actions. If a Christian is truly committed to Jesus Christ and to serving His purposes, then the business will be run according to His principles and precepts. Obviously that means that a Christian must first understand God's rules. Anyone attempting to follow God's plan for business will discover a startling difference between what the world says is normal and what God says is normal. Therefore the committed Christian must accept that he or she is merely a manager of God's business. If God's Word says to do something a particular way, the committed Christian will do it. If the Word says not to do something, then it won't be done. Without a doubt, such decisions potentially can be costly. But the right decisions will yield something greater than money—God's wisdom and peace.

An additional reward that God promises to those who follow Him is prosperity. After all, what kind of witnesses would we be if others saw us fail every time we followed God's rules? Indeed, the opposite is true. God wrote the rules of business economics and, through the ages, those who followed His path have prospered.

"For its profit is better than the profit of silver, and its gain than fine gold. She is more precious then jewels; and nothing you desire compares with her" (Proverbs 3:14-15).

WHAT IS THE TRUE PURPOSE OF BUSINESS?

If a Christian's business is to be used to serve God, it has but one overriding purpose—to glorify Him. Acknowledging that will make decision-making much simpler. Each decision—hiring, firing, paying, promoting, tithing—must be made in harmony with God's written Word. Obviously, God's Spirit leads us day by day but always within the boundaries of what He has chosen to commit to the written Word.

BALANCE IN BUSINESS

The purpose of a Christian's business is to glorify God. The day-by-day functions are the things we do to accomplish that purpose. No one function is more or less important, and each must be done with excellence. For instance, if the business aspects are neglected for the sake of evangelism, quite often the business will fail. If the ministry functions are neglected to generate profits, the business loses its witness in the world.

That certainly can be observed in our society today. Often the term "Christian" in conjunction with a business brings to mind an image of people who don't pay their bills and tell the creditors they are just "trusting the Lord" for their money. On the other hand, many Christian-operated businesses are extremely profitable and are operated honestly and ethically, but few people even know the owner is a Christian. In his or her business life, that person is a "secret service" Christian. Obviously these extremes do not constitute every Christian-run business; however, too few present a balanced image of good business based on biblical principles.

THE FUNCTIONS OF A BUSINESS

There are five basic business functions that constitute the activities of a Christian business.

1. *Evangelism.* No tool is more effective for evangelism than a business dedicated to the Lord. Not only can employees be won by a dedicated

owner or manager but, similarly, so can suppliers, creditors, and customers. The key here is the walk, not the talk.

2. *Discipleship*. Evangelism is sharing Christ's message of salvation with the lost. Discipleship is training Christians to grow stronger in their faith. In a business, that effort should be directed by the owners or managers to the employees immediately under their authority; then they will be able to disciple the others under their authority.

"And the things which you have heard from me in the presence of many witnesses, these entrust to faithful men, who will be able to teach others also" (2 Timothy 2:2).

"That's well and good," you say, "but what if my managers aren't saved?" If they aren't saved, then you simply back up to the first function. The Christian Businessmen's Committee (CBMC) has an excellent program for lifestyle evangelism lifestyle evangelism, ideally suited for developing a witness with managers.

3. *To fund God's work*. A business is the best tool ever created for funding God's work. A properly run business can generate excess capital

9

to meet needs, share the gospel, and still continue its operations day by day. There are many creative ways to use such funds to further God's work. Obviously, giving to your church and to ministries is good and necessary to do God's work but there are many ministries available within the business itself. For instance, several Christians in business have hired full-time counselors to work with employees who have personal problems. Often, when one business is too small to afford a counselor, several businesses have combined to use a common counselor. Also, many businesses have funds available for needy employees. Others provide cassette tape lending libraries and books as internal ministries to employees.

4. *To provide for needs.* Businesses must provide for the needs of the employees, creditors, customers, and owners. That is done by paying salaries, paying for supplies and equipment in a timely fashion, and providing quality products at fair prices. In our modern business environment, the principle seems to be to meet the owner's needs, wants, and desires first, then pay the employees what is necessary to keep them pla-

cated. Many creditors are paid late or not at all, and the customers are viewed as a necessary evil.

If a Christian business owner accepts meeting needs as a normal part of God's plan, that business will play an effective role in evangelism and discipleship. When employees know that those in authority put the needs of others ahead of their own, they will respond.

5. *To generate profits.* Any business must be able to make a profit if it is to continue operations. Sometimes Christians seem to believe that God will bless them supernaturally even if they ignore every pretense of good management. If you believe that, you haven't studied God's Word very thoroughly. God's Word directs us to think and plan. *"The mind of man plans his way, but the Lord directs his steps"* (Proverbs 16:9).

I have counseled enough Christians in business to know that many claim to operate by faith when, instead, they are being slothful. God's Word does not teach us to sit on our hands, waiting for Him to reveal His perfect will. We are to be active. In other words, we are not to be observers of God's plan but participants in it. *"The soul of the sluggard craves and gets nothing, but the soul of the diligent is made fat"* (Proverbs 13:4).

KEYS TO GENERATING A PROFIT

The keys to generating a profit according to the principles in God's Word are not complicated. Some business industry leaders, such as J. C. Penney, R. G. LeTourneau, Stanley Tam, and Walt Meloon, followed these principles and became known not only for their business acumen but also for their Christian witness.

Acknowledge and obey God's eternal wisdom in operating your business. In other words, seek God's counsel first. *"Trust in the Lord with all your heart, and do not lean on your own understanding. In all your ways acknowledge Him, and He will make your paths straight"* (Proverbs 3:5-6).

Too often we seek God's wisdom but then violate the most basic principles taught in His Word. Seek godly counsel in major decisions. Psalm 1:1 tells us, *"How blessed is the man who does not walk in the counsel of the wicked,"* and Proverbs 15:22 says, *"Without consultation, plans are frustrated, but with many counselors they succeed."*

The Purpose of a Business

Outside of God, a man's primary counselor is his wife. Proverbs 31:11 says, *"The heart of her husband trusts in her, and he will have no lack of gain."* That is a resource that few men utilize.

Often, drifting is the result of a lack of accountability. Too many Christian business owners are not really accountable to anyone. An accountability group of three or more godly men who know God's Word will provide the counsel God directs us to seek.

THE PURPOSE OF A BUSINESS

It is enlightening to reflect on what the Bible has to say about business. Many Christians say they have a Christian business, but what does that mean? Obviously the actual business entity is neither Christian nor non-Christian. A Christian business, therefore, is one that is managed by a Christian. The more control this Christian has, the more the business can reflect his or her spiritual values.

It is interesting to see how many Christians would like for God to make them a success so that they can be witnesses for the Lord, and how few really are witnesses once God does bless them. Clearly, a Christian in business can be used by the Lord but only if the correct priorities have been preestablished. One key to being useful to the Lord is making decisions on the basis of God's Word and not on circumstances, feelings, or society's acceptance.

THE PURPOSE OF A CHRISTIAN'S BUSINESS

The purpose of any Christian in business is to glorify God, not just to make a profit. *"Whatever you do, do your work heartily, as for the Lord rather than for men"* (Colossians 3:23).

As in any other area of service, it is important to establish a priority system. We can become so involved with the urgent things of this world that we neglect the important things. Early in a business career, the urgent thing is to make payroll. Later it becomes urgent to make a greater profit or build a bigger company.

Therefore, it is important always to strive for balance in business. That is true in a spiritual sense as well as in a material sense. For example, sales are important to any business, but if a manufacturing company applies 100 percent of its labor force to sales, the imbalance will be readily apparent. One priority of a business should be to lead others to the Lord. However, if all other functions are ignored in pursuit of evangelism, the work will be short lived. So your priority should be to set goals and then be sure your goals are balanced to achieve the overall objective of serving God while meeting material needs.

Goal 1: Salvation. Compared to eternity, the profile of a business is rather trivial and a lifetime of work rather insignificant. If used wisely, though, a business can change the lives of countless unsaved people. When the primary thrust of a business person's outreach is to ensure that others within his or her sphere of influence hear the promises of Jesus Christ, that person's efforts take on a whole new perspective. There is an old cliché that seems applicable here: "If it doesn't work in your life, don't export it." Nothing speaks louder than a phony, and nothing will turn others off more than a business person who lives carnally and talks spiritually. However, if we wait until we're perfect, we'll never share

Christ's claims. God expects application, not perfection.

No group is more accessible to a business owner than the company's employees. It never ceases to amaze me that a business person will spend thousands of dollars to travel around the world to speak to lost people about Christ, when there are many unsaved in his or her own business who have never heard the truth. Often it is the fear of rejection that makes us first seek out those we don't know.

Once the message has been taken to the employees in an inoffensive manner, then it should be presented to others, such as suppliers, peers, and customers. Sharing Christ with others through the business environment should not be done under compulsion, nor should witnessing be used as a club. God prepares the hearts of men through the Holy Spirit and then provides the opportunity to share in a meaningful way.

A forced sharing is what we do for God; fruitful sharing is what God does through us. It is important to keep in mind that in the daily routine of operating a business "as unto the Lord," God will provide these opportunities to share. It is not necessary to sacrifice good business practices, and consequently the business, in order to serve the Lord. Satan would have us believe that serving the Lord requires abandoning good common sense. Indeed, serving the Lord *provides* good common sense.

"Then you will discern the fear of the Lord, and discover the knowledge of God. For the Lord gives wisdom; from His mouth come knowledge and understanding" (Proverbs 2:5-6).

Goal 2: Use of funds. The first use of funds is to honor the Lord. Proverbs 3:9 says, *"Honor the Lord from your wealth, and from the first of all your produce."*

We can look at these Scriptures from any perspective, and they still say the same thing: God wants the first part of our increase. That is not a requirement; it is a promise. It is God's promise that if we honor Him materially before the world, He will in turn honor us. Literally, we acknowledge His lordship. If Christ is Lord, then He is owner as well; our money is His to preserve or disburse as He sees fit. We only manage it for Him until He returns. Therefore the firstfruits from any business should be surrendered in the name of the Lord. Where, how, and how much?

That is a subject for a later principle.

The second use of funds from a business is to meet the needs of its employees. In Deuteronomy 17:15-20 God establishes the standards for His leaders. One is to live moderately. Those who do not observe this simple rule often lose sensitivity for others who have less, and many become callous and corrupt. Any Christian intent on serving the Lord must keep in mind Christ's example to the world.

"But Jesus called them to Himself, and said, 'You know that the rulers of the Gentiles lord it over them, and their great men exercise authority over them. It is not so among you, but whoever wishes to become great among you shall be your servant, and whoever wishes to be first among you shall be your slave'" (Matthew 20:25-27).

To mortals, authority and position mean power and wealth. To God, they mean responsibility. A Christian business person who seeks to serve the Lord will also deal fairly with those faithful employees who helped to build the business.

The third use of funds is to pay suppliers and creditors on time. There is no poorer witness than a Christian who is consistently delinquent on accounts. It is the responsibility of every Christian in business to budget wisely and live on surplus funds instead of accounts payable. Many businesses operate on the principle "I'll pay when and if it's convenient." They ride their creditors to the limit, believing that it is easier to owe someone else than to cut back during tough times. *"Do not withhold good from those to whom it is due, when it is in your power to do it. Do not say to your neighbor, 'Go, and come back, and tomorrow I will give it,' when you have it with you"* (Proverbs 3:27-28).

Goal 3: Discipleship. Once the goals for witnessing and the use of money have been determined, the next goal is to disciple those who have been won to the Lord. Obviously, for spiritual growth new Christians must be directed into a sound, Bible teaching church. But to help them become witnesses in the business environment requires some specialized training. The same principles that have become a part of your life should be ingrained within them.

"And the things which you have heard from me in the presence of many witnesses, these entrust to faithful

men, who will be able to teach others also" (2 Timothy 2:2). It is difficult to share Christ in a meaningful way in any relationship. That difficulty is amplified even more for the salesperson in someone else's office. That does not mean we should abandon witnessing; it means that our sensitivity to the leading of the Holy Spirit is vital. Many times young, exuberant, and ill-trained Christians leave a trail of disaster behind them. Instead of picking the ripe fruit, they mow down everything in their paths. Obviously the other danger is that a new believer will be timid to the point of becoming a "secret service" Christian.

A sound discipleship program is a good beginning. The teaching can be accomplished through written materials, audio, or video, but an essential element to the program's success will be the extent of personal follow-up and accountability. Every new disciple ideally should spend several months in a study plan where he or she meets regularly with one other person to discuss victories and defeats.

Does all of this sound difficult and time-consuming? No doubt about it; God's way does not equate success with large numbers. The first step is to start with one or two who are truly seeking God's best. Once they are trained, they can help train others. In our society of instant potatoes and Minute Rice, God still prepares Christians the old-fashioned way—over a period of time.

THE PRINCIPLE OF SUCCESS

I would trust that by now your image of a successful Christian business owner or manager has changed somewhat. Although it's true that one essential element of a Christian business is profit, that is not the most important element. Many unsaved and uncaring men and women have developed profitable businesses without the slightest regard for God. No, to qualify for God's round table requires much higher standards than just net profits. Consider these questions:

1. When people think of you, do they focus on your business success first or your visible image as a disciple of Jesus Christ?
2. Do your employees and close business contacts know and respect your unwavering stand for the Lord and His principles?

3. Does your family receive a fair share of your time and view the business as a ministry as well?
4. Are the bills paid on time and debts kept within the ability of your business to pay?
5. Does the Lord's work receive the best (firstfruits) from the business?
6. Does the business produce a good product or service at a fair price from the customer's perspective?
7. Does the business generate a reasonable profit to continue operating?

"For to a person who is good in His sight He has given wisdom and knowledge and joy, while to the sinner He has given the task of gathering and collecting so that He may give to one who is good in God's sight. This too is vanity and striving after wind" (Ecclesiastes 2:26).

UNEQUALLY YOKED

As always, a study of a particular principle from God's Word must begin with two pertinent questions: What does God's Word say about the subject and why? In 2 Corinthians 6:14 Paul writes, *"Do not be bound together with unbelievers; for what partnership have righteousness and lawlessness, or what fellowship has light with darkness?"* Clearly the "what" is specific in that believers are admonished not to be yoked to nonbelievers. But then other questions arise. What is a yoke, and how far does the principle extend? Does it cover only marriages or extend also to business relationships?

These questions can only be answered by knowing the answer to our second primary question: Why? I trust that you will discover, as I did, that the reason such an instruction is given to Christians is clear. We are to operate with a value system so different from the non-believing world that on a day-by-day basis we will be in conflict with the norm. Our purpose in life is to glorify God in every decision and every action. A non-Christian could not and would not accept decisions made from that perspective. However, before I get ahead of myself and discuss the "why," let's look at the "what" from God's Word.

WHAT IS A YOKE?

Two distinct types of yokes are presented in the Scriptures. One is a collar used on slaves to show their total subjugation. The second, which is of concern here, is a harness used to link two working animals together. In 2 Corinthians 6:14 (NIV) when Paul says, *"Do not be yoked together with unbelievers,"* the yoke referred to is a farm implement.

The yoke was a common everyday device used to couple oxen together for plowing or hauling. The oxen were matched as closely as possible so the burden would be distributed equally. The two animals had to be trained to work together, even walking stride for stride so that the heavy wooden bar would not rub the skin off of their backs as they worked.

Once connected by the yoke, the oxen were no longer two who could choose to go their own way; rather, they became one working unit. It was extremely critical that the yoked animals be closely matched in size, strength, and temperament. If one animal was larger, the weight of the yoke rested upon the smaller and fatigued it rapidly. If one was much stronger, he pulled the bulk of the attached load and would also tire more quickly. And even with two physically matched animals, if one would not yield to the task (and kicked against the traces), then the obedient animal suffered some whiplashes as the owner disciplined the wayward one. The yoke bound them together for the purpose of accomplishing a task, and without mutual compromise it could not be done.

Hence, the analogy of a yoke to a marriage is an accurate one. A marriage should be two people pulling in common bond toward compatible goals and sharing the load equally.

WHEN TO AVOID A YOKE

People with opposite goals and values will not be compatible. When they are linked together, either in marriage or business, their differing values will ultimately create conflicts. As Christians we are admonished not to be yoked together with unbelievers, because the very purpose of our lives will be sidetracked.

When decisions must be made that involve spiritual principles, the unbeliever cannot be expected to be motivated by God's Spirit. Even elementary decisions, such as giving to the Lord, become sources of friction in an unequally yoked relationship.

A FINANCIAL YOKE

It is necessary to take the broad principle of a yoke and narrow down its applicability to the area of finances. But first we must look at what does *not* constitute a yoked relationship.

Employee/employer. When two or more people are related in a work situation by employee-employer agreement, they are not yoked. There is an authority relationship but they are not bound together by either verbal or written agreement (see Titus 3:1; Ephesians 6:5; Colossians 3:22). They are not expected to carry the same load, and either party is free to terminate the relationship according to the predetermined agreement.

Stock ownership. Normally stock ownership would not create a yoke. The stockholder is not bound to the company, except to the limit of financial risk. Actually, there is an authority relationship but the authority rests in the hands of the stockholder. There is no attempt to create a binding, equal relationship. However, each relationship must be reviewed individually. If the intent is to create an equal, binding relationship between two or more people, then a yoke exists.

Other than a marriage, there is no better defined yoke between two or more people than a business partnership. The intent of a partnership is to create a binding relationship where all parties are equal in responsibility, authority, and liability. Indeed, the law deals with partnerships in this manner. If one partner commits to a business decision, all partners are bound by it.

All of the partners' assets, both business and personal, are jointly and individually pledged. Partnerships are difficult under the best of circumstances but can become completely untenable if all the partners do not have compatible financial and spiritual goals. Indeed, Christians may find themselves in situations in which God chooses to discipline one partner through finances and, therefore, all other partners are equally affected.

It is not necessary to attempt to define every type of contractual relationship dealing with business. The *intent* is the important determination. If the intent is to create an equal and binding relationship, then a yoke is created.

INTENT

There is no absolute method of predetermining what creates a yoke and what does not. Marriages and partnerships fit the description of yokes nearly perfectly, so in those cases we are admonished not to be bound to unbelievers. The admonition for Christians not to be yoked to unbelievers should not imply that nonbelievers are less honest people. The principle is given because believers and nonbelievers are not working toward the same ultimate goals. Believers must be willing to pay any price to serve God, while unbelievers will not be willing to do so. Thus their attitudes are incompatible and, ultimately, they will clash.

When a believer and a nonbeliever can maintain a partnership without conflict over the spiritual goals of the company, it is normally because the believer has compromised God's principles (see Romans 12:2).

NOT ALL THINGS ARE PROFITABLE

Just because we can have partnerships with other believers does not mean that we should. Paul said, *"All things are lawful for me, but not all things are profitable"* (1 Corinthians 6:12). Stretching that principle a little, we can say, "Any two Christians can be partners, but not all should be." There are different levels of maturity, commitment, and human compatibility. Choosing a business partner should be done with the same caution with which you would choose a spouse.

EXISTING PARTNERSHIPS

If you are already in an unequally yoked business situation, observe the principles taught by Paul in 1 Corinthians 7. If you have the opportunity to be released from the partnership, you should arrange to be. But if you don't have the opportunity, make your partner's salvation your number one item of prayer. A general observation I would add is that through the consistently godly lifestyle of a Christian partner, an unsaved partner will often decide either to join God's family or to sever the partnership.

MAKING A VOW

It is clear in God's Word that a vow of any kind is not to be taken lightly. Once someone has given his or her word, it becomes a binding contract to be fulfilled. Thus, before agreeing to any terms, it is assumed that an individual has carefully considered the consequences.

For the current generation, that concept is rarely taught and seldom applied. A vow is deemed to be a promise made under one set of circumstances, which may be broken under another. Thus sometimes a vow to pay a creditor is ignored when the usefulness of the product wears out. Indeed, all creditors can be avoided by a perfectly legal arrangement called bankruptcy, if necessary.

When a couple gets married, they exchange vows or promises to each other. They promise to love each other and forsake all others, no matter what. That vow is binding even if the other partner becomes a drunk, a thief, disabled, ugly, or old. Today, though, the common attitude is "If it doesn't work out, I can always get out," and usually that's what happens. The original conditions that made the promises seem legitimate change, and one partner begins to think he or she should have negotiated a better "deal."

LEGAL LOOPHOLES

The more prevalent this attitude becomes, the trickier contracts or vows become. Most people try to leave loopholes so that if they change their minds they can get out. Then the vows become clouded with attorneys and legal jargon, and a simple contract becomes the meeting ground for adversaries.

GOD'S PROMISES

The reason most Christians are not able to claim God's promises is because they are not willing to meet His prerequisites. First John 3:21-22 explains that God will answer our prayers when we do the things that are pleasing in His sight and keep His commandments. Few scriptural principles are clearer than that of keeping our vows—literally keeping our word both to God and to others. *"It is better that you should not vow than that you should vow and not pay"* (Ecclesiastes 5:5).

HONESTY

All Christians' usefulness to God is directly proportional to their honesty. When we give our word and then go back on it, we have changed our "yes" to "no" and our "no" to "yes." *"He who walks in his uprightness fears the Lord, but he who is*

crooked in his ways despises Him"
(Proverbs 14:2).

Honesty goes beyond not telling
an outright lie; it must include being
reliable to fulfill promises made.
God's Word calls that loyalty. A
Christian's loyalty is not ultimately
to another person; indeed, few people
are really deserving of our uncompromising loyalty. Our loyalty is to
God and to His Word. In being loyal
to Him, we become instruments for
God to show others His loyalty. It
would be a tough life for us if God
changed His mind whenever the
"deal" wasn't right. Our only hope
rests in the fact that God is loyal to
His promises, regardless of how bad
His end of the deal is.

*"Many a man proclaims his own
loyalty, but who can find a trustworthy
man? A righteous man who walks in
his integrity—How blessed are his sons
after him"* (Proverbs 20:6-7).

PRIDE

The opposite of humility is pride.
Pride is perhaps the major sin in
Christendom today. Pride—the desire
to be first—leads to greed, a craving
for more. When someone fails to keep
a vow that has been made in good

faith, it is usually either because of pride or because of greed. The problem lies in the fact that when someone dishonors an agreement just for personal gain, he or she is the real loser. More money won't help replace what's been lost: integrity.

"Everyone who is proud in heart is an abomination to the Lord; assuredly, he will not be unpunished" (Proverbs 16:5).

TRUST

Many times Christians read through the Bible without grasping the fact that it is a handbook for life. God's Word says that we will be accountable for our words and actions on the day of judgment. Jesus Christ said that our motives are shown by our decisions about money. Many compromising Christians are going to be saddened to learn that their treasures were just wood, hay, and stubble. When it really counted, they couldn't be trusted in a small thing, so God never used them in larger things.

"No one can serve two masters; for either he will hate the one and love the other, or he will hold to one and despise the other. You cannot serve God and mammon" (Matthew 6:24).

Sound Business Principles

We are so conscious of our rights today that I believe our rights will ultimately cost us our freedom. In the area of contracts, many people believe it's their right to strike a better deal later if the circumstances change. What about our responsibilities? The word means to be accountable for our actions. Christ said His followers must be willing to surrender their rights and become His stand-ins. It is inconceivable to think that our Lord would make an agreement with someone and then change His mind and try to negotiate a better deal. As a carpenter, I rather imagine Jesus delivered His products at the negotiated prices, regardless of what His costs were or what the market was doing.

In Matthew, Jesus gives us just such an example of being satisfied with a bargain once struck. Various workers were hired during the day at an agreed-upon sum, which happened to be exactly the same amount for each worker. At the end of the day those who had worked all day for the same wages as those who had worked only one hour were grumbling at the landowner because they felt they had

34

been cheated. The landowner's response was, *"Friend, I am doing you no wrong; did you not agree with me for a denarius?"* (Matthew 20:13). The issue wasn't whether or not the wage was sufficient—it was just that someone else got a better deal, and that wasn't "right."

WHAT WE DESERVE

The one certain rule of contract law is that once a contract is made, one party can't arbitrarily decide to modify or cancel it. Christians can be truly thankful that God's contract with us is binding and firm. Otherwise He might give us what we deserve. However, God says that if we wish to be forgiven, we must forgive others. If we wish to exercise God's promise to call upon Him in our day of trial, we must pay our vows.

"Offer to God a sacrifice of thanksgiving, and pay your vows to the Most High; and call upon Me in the day of trouble; I shall rescue you, and you will honor Me" (Psalms 50:14-15).

AUTHORITY

Once Christians have agreed to submit to an authority, as in the case of professional athletes under contract, they are admonished to give honor to that authority, even if the authority doesn't deserve it. Clearly the apostle Paul did not condone or approve of slavery, but in Ephesians 6:5 he admonishes Christian slaves to be obedient to their masters and not to give eyeservice, but to do their work sincerely, as unto Christ. When a Christian honors authority, God promises that rewards will come from the Lord. *"Knowing that whatever good thing each one does, this he will receive back from the Lord, whether slave or free"* (Ephesians 6:8).

In conclusion, James puts it into proper perspective: *"But prove yourselves doers of the Word, and not merely hearers who delude themselves"* (James 1:22), and, *"Therefore, to one who knows the right thing to do, and does not do it, to him it is sin"* (James 4:17). As believers we should determine before the Lord what vows we have made and, in each case, be willing to fulfill them—regardless!

FINANCIAL HONESTY

Recently a businessman asked me, "Do you think it's possible to be totally honest in our business society?" Since that particular individual was a committed Christian, I had no doubt that his question was an honest one. He went on to explain that he didn't purposely cheat anyone, but even when negotiating a sale the common practice was for the seller to begin at a price higher than desired, knowing that the buyer always started with a price lower than he knew was acceptable. As I considered his question, I realized what he had asked must be a conscious thought on the hearts of many sincere Christians: "Can you truly be honest and, if so, at what cost?"

MONEY IS AN INDICATOR

The Lord says in Luke 16:10, *"He who is faithful in a very little thing is faithful also in much."* The small thing to which the Lord is referring is money. Naturally, this also includes the pursuit of money.

God has placed us in a physical world and expects us to live in it. Why is that? God could miraculously provide for us on a day-by-day basis if He chose to do so. Why then has He determined to leave us in a materialistic society, subject to the same problems and temptations as those who totally reject His ways? After all, the one who truly seeks to follow God's will surely will suffer at the hands of those who live only to please themselves.

The answer becomes clear in the light of God's Word. In Philippians 2:15 Paul tells us to hold ourselves above this wicked generation so that we can prove ourselves blameless. Thus we become lights in a world of darkness. We are placed in this society by God so that He can reveal Himself through us. For this to happen, we must avoid the devices of the accuser and hold to the Lord's standards.

Satan works through guile and selfishness and labels them "shrewdness" and "ingenuity." God calls guile "deceit" and selfishness "greed." *"He who winks his eyes does so to devise perverse things"* (Proverbs 16:30). *"For where jealousy and selfish ambition exist, there is disorder and every evil thing"* (James 3:16).

WHY THE DISHONEST PROSPER

There is little doubt that, in the short run, a deceitful person will seem to prosper. But it doesn't take long for others to recognize his dishonesty, so he must continually seek out new prospects. Sometimes the deceitful person may gain materially as a result of his craftiness. We must remember that Satan does have limited authority over this earth and can indeed provide riches. The problem with his supply is that it is always accompanied by fear, anxiety, anger, greed, and resentment.

Every Christian must accept God's Word as the standard for doing business. Only the Lord's provision brings with it peace and contentment (see Proverbs 3:4-6; 10:22). It is also within God's power to grant material blessings to those who truly follow His directions. *"Riches and honor are with me, enduring wealth and righteousness"* (Proverbs 8:18). But many times God elects to store those riches for distribution in eternity, in which case the rewards are multiplied a thousandfold (see Matthew 6:20).

The biggest loss associated with following the worldly path is the loss of God's full blessing. Many Christians fail to experience God's blessing because they conform to the image of the world (see Romans 12:2).

God declares that if we do not re-spond correctly in such a trivial thing as money, we will not be en-trusted with any greater possessions. *"If therefore you have not been faithful in the use of unrighteous mammon, who will entrust the true riches to you?"* (Luke 16:11).

MATERIAL WITNESS

It becomes clear that God has placed us in this materialistic world not only to witness to the unsaved but also for the purpose of examining our relationship to Him. There can be no clearer reflection of our true value system than the way we handle our money and the way we treat oth-ers when profit or loss is involved.

Can Christians be honest in our society? We must be to experience the fullness of God's power and love. There will be times when it will seem that others take advantage of that honesty. The Lord knew that would happen. *"If anyone wishes to come af-ter Me, let him deny himself, and take up his cross daily and follow Me"* (Luke 9:23). Often there is a price to be paid for following in the path of Christ, but there is also a great re-ward as a result of doing so.

Financial Honesty

The Lord tells us that a house built upon sand will fall when the storms come, while one built upon the rock will survive. We are in the midst of a materialistic storm today, and every Christian must decide whether to build upon the solid rock of God's Word or the shifting sands of society. The decision to do business by the world's normal standards—guile and deception—is a decision to deny Christ. *"No servant can serve two masters; for either he will hate the one, and love the other, or else he will hold to one and despise the other. You cannot serve God and mammon"* (Luke 16:13).

OBEDIENCE TO GOD

The principle taught throughout the Scripture is: We don't serve God because of what He can do for us; we serve Him because He is God. Job understood this principle when he told his friends, *"Though He slay me, I will hope in Him"* (Job 13:15).

Nebuchadnezzar, about to cast Shadrach, Meshach, and Abednego into the furnace because they did not worship the idol he chose, mocked God by saying, *"What god is there who can deliver you out of my hands?"*

(Daniel 3:15). The three men responded, *"If it be so, our God whom we serve is able to deliver us from the furnace of blazing fire; and He will deliver us out of your hand, O king. But even if He does not, let it be known to you, O king, that we are not going to serve your gods or worship the golden image that you have set up"* (Daniel 3:17-18).

Each Christian must come to the position where God's approval is more important than the world's riches. Then, and only then, will the full measure of God's peace and power be experienced. *"But prove yourselves doers of the Word, and not merely hearers who delude themselves"* (James 1:22).

BUSINESS ETHICS

Perhaps nothing reflects the decline of our society more than the state of current business ethics. It is not at all uncommon to read about major companies paying bribes to government officials or providing large kickbacks to company purchasing agents.

On a smaller scale, many sales companies offer incentives to buyers from other businesses in the form of coupons for merchandise, vacations, cash, or Christmas gifts. These are available on a voluntary basis, in spite of the fact that nearly every company has established rules against their purchasing agents accepting such items. *"A wicked man receives a bribe from the bosom to pervert the ways of justice"* (Proverbs 17:23).

THE COST OF COMPROMISE

There is a price to be paid for every compromise, especially to God's Word. That price is the loss of peace from God. Compromise at any level results in further compromise until finally the conscience is seared and right and wrong are no longer distinguishable. *"And just as they did not see fit to acknowledge God any longer, God gave them over to a depraved mind, to do those things which are not proper"* (Romans 1:28). An employee who will pad his expense account and rationalize it will eventually pad his income and rationalize that as well. *"Bread obtained by falsehood is sweet to a man, but afterward his mouth will be filled with gravel"* (Proverbs 20:17).

Fortunately, nobody is worthy before God. Our greatest advantage is the fact that God doesn't have much talent to work with down here. He will restore anyone who will acknowledge his or her sin and return to His way. If God commanded us to forgive each other seven times a day (Luke 17:4), how much more will He forgive us? *"If we confess our sins, He is faithful and righteous to forgive us our sins and to cleanse us from all unrighteousness"* (1 John 1:9).

BECOMING A LIGHT

In our society most people are looking for guidance and unwavering commitment to principles. Unfortunately, when these can't be found, many people are duped by the humanist's argument that "values are established by society." The end result of this lie can be seen in the abuses of our day—drugs used to escape reality, sexual immorality, a high rate of divorce—and ultimately in the collapse of society itself.

Why did people turn to enslavement through a form of government such as Communism? It was because it offered an uncompromising set of principles that seem to represent stability. In reality, only Christ assures both stability and love.

It is the responsibility of every believer to adhere uncompromisingly to the set of values presented in God's Word. These values encompass the business as well as the personal life. A Christian must decide either to follow Christ or to follow Satan. There is no middle road. A business will be dedicated to the furtherance of either God's kingdom or Satan's. If the primary purpose of a Christian in business is to be a success and make money, then God's way is not for that person. Christ promised that following His way would be costly. *"And He was saying to them all, 'If anyone wishes to come after Me, let him deny himself, and take up his cross daily and follow Me'"* (Luke 9:23).

Certainly, taking a stand for Christ won't always be admired because it will cause a great deal of discomfort to those who know of Him but don't serve Him. Christ Himself said He came not to bring peace but division—not a division based on pride, position, or anger, but on principle. The liars and the thieves will cheat those who obey godly principles, and it is quite possible that the ways of the wicked will cause them to prosper. A Christian must remember that all that is seen is not all that there is. *"The wicked earns deceptive wages, but he who sows righteousness gets a true reward"* (Proverbs 11:18).

BUSINESS GOALS

For a Christian in business the number one goal must be to share Christ with others. The business is merely a tool to reach people who may never be reached otherwise. The method will vary according to the business and the number of employees. One business owner may choose to call the employees in and witness to them. Another may use an outsider to speak in a weekly devotional.

The next step should be a plan for regular fellowship through a company devotional time, which employees are invited, but not pressured, to attend. The important principle is to take a stand and present Christ's message (see Colossians 1:28). Once a plan has been implemented for sharing with employees, the next step is to share the message with suppliers and customers.

In addition to the spiritual goals established, company owners should have some straightforward business goals. If their goals are merely to make a lot of money, build a lot of buildings, and leave it all to their children, how are the goals different from those of non-Christians?

1. *Pay a fair wage.* Many Christian employees are guilty of paying some employees less than a livable wage. To hire someone at such a low wage is in direct violation of the principle of fairness. *"You shall not oppress a hired servant who is poor and needy, whether he is one of your countrymen or one of your aliens who is in your land in your towns"* (Deuteronomy 24:14).

To pay less than what is needed to live reasonably well places the employee in a position of not being able to provide for his or her family. If a job will not support a livable wage for someone with a family, then do not hire anyone who has a family, for doing so will result in short-term, disgruntled employees.

2. *Build a good product.* "A good name is to be more desired than great riches, favor is better than silver and

gold" (Proverbs 22:1). A company is known by the quality of its products or service. What a great witness it would be if every time a customer encountered a Christian-operated company what was remembered was the quality of service.

3. *Make a fair profit.* It is an interesting observation that the primary thing that holds prices in line, even for Christian businesses, is competition. In a situation where little or no competition exists, most Christian business people will escalate prices until buyer demand drops off. Such pricing sounds like good business. But is it scriptural? *"Better is a little with righteousness than great income with injustice"* (Proverbs 16:8). Should a Christian in business, whether offering a factory product or a doctor's services, charge what the traffic will bear? Wouldn't it be a testimony to the Lord and His people if Christians established prices and fees on the basis of what is fair both for them and for their customers?

4. *Be a godly leader.* *"Where there is no guidance, the people fall, but in abundance of counselors there is victory"* (Proverbs 11:14). Above all else, a Christian employer should be a god-

ly leader. That means a life free from sin and corruption. Too often Christians are guilty of hypocrisy by taking a stand outside the business environment but not living it inside the company.

PURPOSE OF BUSINESS

Does that mean then that Christians are supposed to be losers and never be successful? Obviously not, but priorities must be established outside of what the world calls success. Christ warned us that we could gain the entire world and forfeit our souls in the pursuit of it. The purposes of Christians in business are the same as that of any other Christians—to glorify God and to lead others to Christ.

A business is nothing more than a tool to accomplish God's work. Making money and acquiring success are by-products of putting God first (see Matthew 6:33). Both employees and employers need to take a stand based on God's Word and become lights to their unsaved counterparts. Will such a stand cost business? Almost beyond a doubt it will—initially. For some employees it may even cost them their jobs, if those jobs include bribes and other types of deceit. However, God's Word promises that He owns everything and that He delights in helping those who completely sell out to Him. *"For the eyes of the Lord move to and fro throughout the earth that He may strongly support those whose heart is completely His"* (2 Chronicles 16:9).

COST OF COMMITMENT

It is not necessary to speak of Christ with everyone you meet in order to serve the Lord. Obviously there are situations in which witnessing is not possible or productive. However, being a "silent witness" is a rationalization for being no witness at all. If Christ is first in your life, you will share Him with others. Wisdom will determine the method; the Holy Spirit will provide the opportunity. If you are an employee who is restricted by employer rules, it may mean using dinners or other opportunities outside of business hours. If you are an employer, it means using every available opportunity to glorify Christ in words and in actions, both to your employees and to your customers.

I recall a story that a Christian businessman told me about one of his key employees. That employee had secretly been praying for God to touch him and heal him of a desire for other women. The employee suffered a divorce and an emotional breakdown that led him from one counselor to another and ultimately to an attempt at suicide. After nearly three years of depression, he came in one day, elated to announce that he had found Christ as his Savior and had turned his life over to Him. The company president congratulated him and revealed that he also was a Christian and had been praying for him. To this the employee exclaimed, "Why didn't you tell me where you got your strength and peace? I just thought it was because you owned the company."

PAYING A FAIR WAGE

I once asked a group of Christian employers, "How much should a Christian employer pay employees?" The answer ranged from minimum wage, as a legal requirement, to a large bonus for special employees; but not a single answer was confirmed on the basis of our source of truth—God's Word. Those Christian employers weren't just run-of-the-mill Christians, either. They were mostly dedicated men and women seeking to do God's will, as well as they knew it.

The difficulty is that in our generation, and in many previous generations, we have been conformed to the image of our world. In fact, in most instances we are indistinguishable in our daily activities. Our words may be different, but our faith is not always reflected through our works. I find that many Christian employers take an identical approach toward employee wages as do most non-Christian employers.

BUSINESS CYCLES

Anyone who has read much business history recognizes that management attitudes go in cycles. When business is depressed and jobs are few, the managers and owners call the shots, and labor really can't do much about it. During those times wages are often cut, benefits are cut, and most new employees are recruited at reduced wages. Then the cycle reverses, business gets very good, trained labor is in short supply, and wages are forced up by organized labor unions.

Prior to the twentieth century, the cycles affected relatively few industries. Today, with mass media, they develop quickly and in virtually every area of business. What we have developed is a traditional adversary relationship between owners and workers in which each tries to exploit the other whenever possible.

THE PRINCIPLES OF FAIR PAY

I believe the overwhelming principle about paying employees according to God's Word is fairness, but not fairness according to the *world's* standards. God is not concerned with what others think is fair, only with what He thinks is fair. If you were to review all the passages dealing with paying employees and boil them down to a simple principle, I believe you would be left with two options regarding pay. You must either pay employees what they need to live on or hire only those who can live on what you're able to pay.

Once someone is in your employ, as a Christian you are obligated to meet his or her basic needs to the limit of your ability to do so. Quite obviously, then, each employee's need level must be determined. Arriving at an actual dollar amount is difficult, but I have found some fundamental steps helpful.

Survey your employees to determine if they feel that they are making enough to live on. Then have an experienced, qualified financial counselor work with them to develop a minimum family budget. Review that budget yourself, and simply put yourself in the employee's position to see if you could live on it.

WHAT CAN YOU PAY?

Obviously some businesses do so poorly that paying adequate salaries is not always possible. If that situation continues over an extended period of time, however, there has to be some doubt about the wisdom of continuing the operation. If God can direct by supplying, He can also direct by withholding. Perhaps the most obvious examples of this are some Christian organizations—most notable in recent years, Christian schools. Many of them pay so poorly (and seldom) that almost no one other than the administration can live above the poverty level. If God has truly directed this effort, then adequate salaries should be the norm.

More often than not, the failure of most businesses to pay adequate salaries at the lowest levels is really one of choice rather than necessity. If you look at the assets of the company, the salaries of management, and particularly the indulgences of the owners, most often there is more than enough for the lowest paid employees to be paid fairly.

Secular business philosophy teaches that "to the victor belong the spoils." That translates into a trait the Bible calls selfishness. *He who shuts his ear to the cry of the poor will also cry himself and not be answered"* (Proverbs 21:13).

It is important for a Christian employer to review every attitude in the light of God's Word to determine if it meets God's minimum. It would be very difficult to stand before a group of employees and testify that you are a Christian and want to operate your business by Christian principles while many of them can't meet even the basic needs of their families. (Of course, you are not responsible if their financial problems are caused by their own indulgences.)

WHOSE NEEDS COME FIRST?

A commonly practiced but seldom expressed principle of management today is to do what you have to do to keep the employees pacified. In other words, respond according to the pressure they exert; thus, most wage negotiations become battles between adversaries. That has never been part of God's direction for meeting needs and building businesses. And that is exactly why we are now studying Japanese management to conclude why they are more productive. Their success really isn't difficult to understand—they simply built a management system around a biblical principle known as caring.

"Do nothing from selfishness or empty conceit, but with humility of mind let each of you regard one another as more important than himself; do not merely look out for your own personal interests, but also for the interests of others" (Philippians 2:3-4).

Since the Japanese don't have business management schools to teach that principle, it must be applied at the root level—face to face. They don't allow an "us against them" attitude in management. Instead, each employee shares in the financial success of the company.

If Christianity simply practiced what God's Word teaches on this subject, the world would be studying our management techniques, because we would have contented employees sharing in the most profitable businesses in the world. Instead, we are virtually indistinguishable from the world.

SCRIPTURAL WARNING

God's Word offers some sober counsel to believers who fit into the worldly model of indulging themselves while others in their care suffer. Deuteronomy 17 describes the kind of leader God desires for His people. The same characteristics would apply to a leader today.

"Moreover, he shall not multiply horses for himself . . . nor shall he greatly increase silver and gold for himself" (Deuteronomy 17:16-17).

James amplifies this and, in the blunt language of a prophet, describes those who would act selfishly. *"Come now, you rich, weep and howl for your miseries which are coming upon you. . . . Behold, the pay of the la-*

borers who mowed your fields, and which has been withheld by you, cries out against you; and the outcry of those who did the harvesting has reached the ears of the Lord of Sabaoth. You have lived luxuriously on the earth and led a life of wanton pleasure; you have fattened your hearts in a day of slaughter" (James 5:1,4-5).

BALANCE

God's Word does not suggest that a Christian employer has to pay the highest wages around and, certainly, not to the detriment of his business. What is required is that at least minimum needs are met and that we are not cheating our workers out of fair wages. No employer will lose by following God's principles for paying people. What you lose in current cash, you make up for in long-term stability. However, too much of a good principle can often backfire. If you pay everyone the maximum amount possible and don't lay aside any surplus funds, then economic cycles will play havoc with the business.

Every phase of a Christian's business must mesh together, and a part of that is anticipating difficulties. We live in a physical world and are subject to natural forces as well. It does not mean God can't or won't intercede on our behalf—He can and often does. But when you set out in a leaky boat, you may get wet. *"There is precious treasure and oil in the dwelling of the wise, but a foolish man swallows it up"* (Proverbs 21:20). Remember that the better the business does, the better everyone does.

SOWING AND REAPING

"Do not be deceived, God is not mocked; for whatever a man sows, this he will also reap" (Galatians 6:7).

The principle of sowing and reaping is usually directly applicable to dealing with other people and since employees are "other people," it applies to them as well. When an employer is able to exercise total control because of prevailing economic circumstances, there is an opportunity to demonstrate with actions what words can never do. Literally, you are sowing attitudes into the lives of others. They will often take root, grow, and return to you, so if you sow love and caring, you reap the same. If you sow indifference and contempt, you'll reap that also.

LET US BE DOERS

Quite often Christian business leaders fall short in the "doing" end of God's Word. I have observed that one reason many Christian business owners travel to give their personal testimony is that they get a rather cool reception at home, where their business practices are known. Obviously you can't please everyone. Whatever you pay, there will be those who don't think it's enough or who will resent the fact that someone else makes more. But the principle is clear: You don't have to please everyone; just please God.

WORK AS UNTO THE LORD

"Whatever you do, do your work heartily, as for the Lord rather than for men; knowing that from the Lord you will receive the reward of inheritance. It is the Lord Christ whom you serve" (Colossians 3:23-24).

In addition to supplying our physical needs, work plays an important role in our spiritual lives. It provides the opportunity to put into practice spiritual principles that would otherwise be mere academics. A Christian can study every passage in the Bible dealing with serving others and read every biography of those who were noted servants, such as George Mueller, and still not really understand the principle of surrendering rights.

On the job, however, the opportunity to yield our rights presents itself every day. The way we do our work provides the best exterior reflection of our commitment to serve the Lord in a genuine, tangible way. It doesn't matter whether that work is in the home, on an assembly line, or in a corporate office. Our true Christian beliefs will be reflected more clearly there than in any other environment outside the immediate family relationships.

The chain of relationships from the family to work is so intertwined that the apostle Paul listed them as a series in Colossians 3: first, husband-wife relationships (verses 18-19); second, parent-children relationships (verses 20-21), and third, authority-work relationships (verses 22-23). Paul knew that unless a Christian had all of those managed properly, life could not manifest joy, peace, or contentment. A great deal of teaching is available now on the first two areas —marriage and children. However, little has been written on an equally large area of difficulty —authority-work relationships.

CURRENT ATTITUDES

For many Christians, work is a necessary evil; for others, it is an area of "worship." Obviously both are extremes and represent a spiritual imbalance.

Many Christians view their jobs as drudgery—just a means to earn money so that they can enjoy themselves. They are dissatisfied with their vocation, disgruntled on the job, and resentful of others' successes. A by-product of all this mental anxiety is quite often fatigue on the job and restlessness at home. To compensate, they fill their lives with endless outside activities. For nonbelievers, these are usually hunting, fishing, boating, skiing, and so on. For the Christian, they may be church activities and civic functions. These activities are not bad in themselves; in fact, they are quite good unless the activities are a substitute for the lack of fulfillment at work.

Somehow Christians have been duped into believing that work is a secular activity and, therefore, one shouldn't expect to feel spiritual about a job. That attitude destroys our greatest area of outreach and witness. Few Christians who view their work as a chore have much of a witness on or off the job. Proverbs 22:29 says, *"Do you see a man skilled in his work? He will stand before kings; he will not stand before obscure men."*

RESENTMENT

It is amazing how clearly spiritual problems are reflected on the job. I once spoke at a company meeting and, afterward, one of the employees cornered me to let me know how oppressed he was. He said that everyone else received bigger raises and better promotions but he always did the most work. He went on and on until I told him I had to go. On the way out, the owner told me he believed the man could be a key employee, but he always had his feelings hurt about decisions even remotely affecting him, and he was resentful of anyone else's recognition. It was obvious that he had a spiritual problem that was being reflected in a physical way.

Such problems are not unique to industry. The leader of a large Christian organization once related that he had less trouble with employees when he was in business than he did in the ministry. He said, "I once naively thought that I could deal with Christian staff differently. On the contrary, in great part they see the other staff members as competitors, and if I do something extra for one, many of the others resent it." It would seem that we have failed to teach Christians that the job is an extension of their walk with the Lord, not isolated from it.

BIBLICAL ADMONITION

It is fortunate for all of us that God's Word is both simple and complete. No subject affecting our lives is left to our own imagination. Those who are resentful about the success of others, whose feelings are hurt because of the lack of recognition, or who use their jobs as their alter egos all suffer from the same spiritual malady—they are in service to people instead of God. Unfortunately, people will always fail; fortunately, God never will. If a Christian approaches a job with the attitude that he or she must be recognized as the best, there will almost always be disappointment, because the first time the boss

forgets to show appreciation, resentment creeps in.

HOW TO BREAK THE TRAP

1. *Be honest.* The first step is to
confess to God that any attitude of resentment, ego, pride, or desire for
praise is unacceptable and needs to
be corrected. First John 1:9 says, *"If
we confess our sins, He is faithful and
righteous to forgive us our sins and to
cleanse us from all unrighteousness."*

2. *Admit openly.* The next step is
to seek the forgiveness of those who
may have been offended or hurt. Acknowledge this as a personal weakness and ask their help in detecting
and correcting it in the future. Galatians 6:2-3 says, *"Bear one another's
burdens, and thus fulfill the law of
Christ. For if anyone thinks he is
something when he is nothing, he de-
ceives himself."* A word of caution is
necessary here. Do not expect everyone to appreciate or understand your
actions. Remember that you serve
Christ, not men. It is for your relationship to Him that you need to correct the problem. That is equally true
of a housewife whose husband and
children seemingly never appreciate

her. Correct your attitudes and actions, and leave the results to God.

3. *Take correct action.* Satan's number one weapon is defeat, but God's number one promise is victory. When you find that the original problems have returned, never allow yourself to dwell on them. Confess them again, publicly if necessary. Many times a little ego deflation is necessary to make a commitment firm. That will also require that you forgive any offense that someone else commits against you. Colossians 3:13 says, *"Bearing with one another, and forgiving each other, whoever has a complaint against any one; just as the Lord forgave you, so also should you."*

4. *Spiritual renewal.* Since the problems are spiritual, the solution must be spiritual also. The only source of spiritual renewal is the Holy Spirit. Examine your daily spiritual life honestly. Do you spend time regularly in prayer and the study of God's Word? Without regular spiritual food, even the most determined Christian will develop spiritual anemia. Group prayer, conferences, and church are not substitutes for a personal relationship with God. If Christ

needed to withdraw and be alone with God, we must also.

Romans 12:2 says, *"And do not be conformed to this world, but be transformed by the renewing of your mind, that you may prove what the will of God is, that which is good and acceptable and perfect."*

How to Identify Business Bondage

Financial bondage applies to more than just indebtedness. Certainly those who owe more than they can pay are in bondage; but those who have a large surplus and live in fear or pride are also in bondage. Literally, financial bondage is any material thing that interferes with our relationship with God. Thus, the individual who has a surplus of $100,000 a year to invest, but spends a lot of time worrying about how to multiply it and protect it, is in as much bondage scripturally as someone who can't pay credit card bills.

The key to whether or not someone lives in bondage is one's attitude. We are servants of the living God, and when material things bind us, we cannot function effectively. *"So that you may walk in a manner worthy of the Lord, to please Him in all respects, bearing fruit in every good work and increasing in the knowledge of God"* (Colossians 1:10).

All of this is to point out that just as financial bondage does not apply merely to debt, neither does business bondage apply only to failure. Christians whose business involvements preempt God's greater plan for their lives are in bondage. And it really doesn't matter that the efforts are materially successful or that large sums are given to God's work. God never has been impressed by our worldly successes. What He wants is our obedience to His will for our lives. *"No one can serve two masters; for either he will hate the one and love the other, or he will hold to one and despise the other. You cannot serve God and mammon"* (Matthew 6:24).

SYMPTOM 1: OVERCOMMITMENT TO WORK OR SUCCESS

"It is vain for you to rise up early, to retire late, to eat the bread of painful labors; for He gives to His beloved even in his sleep" (Psalm 127:2).

Overcommitment is a term that cannot be defined in hours and minutes. One person can work ten hours and still maintain the correct priorities, whereas another may work ten hours on the job physically and then another ten at home. Overcommitment to business is usually a sign of fear—specifically the fear of failure. Most of the time a Christian will rationalize an overcommitment because "it's for my family." However, when put to a vote, most wives and children would decide otherwise.

Perhaps the most graphic consequence of that particular symptom is the swing toward liberalism in our young people. An overcommitted parent can supply things to his children but not direction (and certainly not balance).

SYMPTOM 2:
AN AIR OF SUPERIORITY

"Instruct those who are rich in this present world not to be conceited or to fix their hope on the uncertainty of riches, but on God, who richly supplies us with all things to enjoy" (1 Timothy 6:17).

Any of at least one hundred scriptural references could be used to demonstrate God's view of our human tendency to elevate people because of their worldly successes. It is even worse when Christians begin to adopt an air of superiority because of their stewardship over some of God's resources. There is no greater deterrent to a consistent walk with the Lord than false pride and self-elevation. Unfortunately, there is a common tendency for people in management or ownership to assume these characteristics or symptoms.

Usually an air of superiority begins with the internal attitude that says, "I started this business; I can do what I want to with it," or it can take a more directed course toward people—especially those who are hourly employees. A Christian executive who establishes a social barrier between himself and assembly workers or truck drivers will find that a spiritual barrier exists as well. But that means the Christian executive is in bondage —the bondage of phony superiority.

"For who regards you as superior? And what do you have that you did not receive? But if you did receive it, why do you boast as if you had not received it?" (1 Corinthians 4:7).

Those in positions of authority must exercise great caution to maintain the proper balance. Authority actually means responsibility, according to God's Word. The single example of perfect leadership was Christ. He consistently told His followers that He came to serve, not to be served. By showing kindness and concern, He did not weaken His authority. He knew, as we should, that His authority and position were in God's kingdom. The leaders and followers of His day tried to convince Him to hold Himself above the poor. Not only did He refuse to do it, He condemned the practice.

"But the greatest among you shall be your servant. And whoever exalts himself shall be humbled; and whoever humbles himself shall be exalted" (Matthew 23:11-12).

The question is often asked, "How can I maintain discipline if I get too close to my employees?" The answer is that if they know that you're applying God's principles fairly and consistently, then they will also know that administering justice along with compassion is a part of that plan. Justice without compassion is callousness, and compassion without justice is weakness.

The symptom of superiority is difficult to overcome. Those Christians I know who struggle to overcome it have discovered something in common. As soon as they begin to treat everyone equally and fairly, some obnoxious employee immediately begins to see how much he can get away with. God's Word says not to look down at others, but it doesn't say that work rules can't be enforced. Some of those who resent authority must either be taught to respect that authority or be released.

SYMPTOM VERSUS PROBLEM

The symptom may be an air of superiority, but the problem is either ego or pride. *"Pride goes before destruction, and a haughty spirit before stumbling"* (Proverbs 16:18). The way to deal with pride is to consciously put others first. Certainly it's difficult and, without a doubt, runs contrary to popular business management principles. But God wrote the Book on business management, and if we really believe that everything belongs to Him, then we will believe it is His plan we are to follow. Remember that the purpose of a Christian's business is to glorify God.

SYMPTOM 3:
SELFISHNESS—INDULGENCE

"Come now, you rich, weep and howl for your miseries which are com-

ing upon you. Your riches have rotted and your garments have become moth-eaten" (James 5:1-2). Far too often those who control a business adopt a "me first" attitude. They underpay many employees, establish their own retirement plans without thought to their employees' needs, and reap most of the available surplus for themselves. More often than not the owner will sell out a successful business, realizing a great profit and leaving the employees with little or nothing to show for the years they have invested. Certainly they received their wages, but a Christian has to ask, "Does my responsibility end at payday?"

SYMPTOM VERSUS PROBLEM

The symptom may manifest itself through selfishness and indulgence, but the problem is greed. We all have an inborn attitude of greed—always desiring more. Until this is brought under God's authority, we will not be good stewards. Consequently we settle for trinkets now when God really desires to pour out His blessings upon us. *"You ask and do not receive, because you ask with wrong motives,*

*so that you may spend it on your plea-
sures"* (James 4:3).

SYMPTOM 4:
CONFUSION—DISORGANIZATION

*"The sluggard does not plow after
the autumn, so he begs during the har-
vest and has nothing"* (Proverbs 20:4).
Almost in total contrast to the overcommitted workaholics are those
Christians who apply themselves at
the minimal level. They're content to
operate with sloppy records and poor
work quality, and they exist in a me-
diocre society without a real Christian testimony.

Christians are instructed to be
excellent in everything they do.
*"Whatever you do, do your work heart-
ily as for the Lord rather than for men"*
(Colossians 3:23). That is a part of
our testimony before the unsaved.

God's way is not a cop-out; it is
the best. It is astounding how medi-
ocre society has become. We build
defects into our equipment and ap-
pliances because of shoddy workman-
ship and then wonder why we aren't
competitive. As Christians, we should
accept excellence as our minimum
standard. The quality of our personal
efforts should be so high that the

unsaved around us are drawn to the Lord through our witness. Instead, few Christians really have such a testimony.

Without a doubt, the pursuit of excellence is an attitude that God commands of us. It would be difficult to convince others that Christianity is the only way if the Christians they see are sloppy and in a state of confusion. Usually these conditions result in frustration and anger for the Christians and for those around them.

SYMPTOM VERSUS PROBLEM

The symptom is disorganization, but the underlying problem is slothfulness, which is generally a by-product of a lack of commitment. In other words, it's an "I don't care" attitude. That is so uncharacteristic of a Christian that one would have to question God's leadership in the life of a lazy person. Anyone can have lapses of excellence caused by pressures, health, or overwork, but continual laziness is a sure sign of spiritual problems (see 1 Peter 4:11).

Christian Financial Concepts

Teaching God's Principles of Handling Money

Larry Burkett, founder and president of Christian Financial Concepts, is the best-selling author of more than a dozen books on business and personal finances. He also hosts two radio programs broadcast on hundreds of stations worldwide.

Larry holds degrees in marketing and finance, and for several years served as a manager in the space program at Cape Canaveral, Florida. He also has been vice president of an electronics manufacturing firm. Larry's education, business experience, and solid understanding of God's Word enable him to give practical, Bible-based financial counsel to families, churches, and businesses.

Founded in 1976, Christian Financial Concepts is a nonprofit, nondenominational ministry dedicated to helping God's people gain a clear understanding of how to manage their money according to scriptural principles. Although practical assistance is provided on many levels, the purpose of CFC is simply *to bring glory to God by freeing His people from financial bondage so that they may serve Him to their utmost.*

One major avenue of ministry involves the training of volunteers in budget and debt counseling and linking them with financially troubled families and individuals through a nationwide referral network. CFC also provides financial management seminars and workshops for churches and other groups.

(Formats available include audio, video, video with moderator, and live instruction.) A full line of printed and audio-visual materials related to money management is available through CFC's materials department ([800] 722-1976).

Career Pathways is the career guidance outreach of Christian Financial Concepts (CFC) of Gainesville, Georgia. Since 1976, under the leadership of Larry Burkett, CFC has focused its ministry on teaching biblical principles of handling money. Career Pathways expands CFC's emphasis on stewardship to include stewardship of other talents, i.e., unique gifts, abilities, and personal style of work.

Based on the biblical teaching that God has a purpose for each individual, the Career Pathways program seeks to reaffirm the Christian perspective by revealing how work is really a part of fulfilling God's purpose.

Career Pathways seeks to help individuals discover their talents and career direction by providing education, testing, and feedback. More than 6,000 people, ages 16-72, have received individualized assessments through the Career Pathways program.

For further information about the ministry of Christian Financial Concepts, write to:

Christian Financial Concepts
P.O. Box 2377
Gainesville, GA 30503-2377

Other Materials by Larry Burkett:

Books in This Series:

Financial Freedom
The Financial Sampler
Giving and Tithing
Insurance Plans
Major Purchases
Personal Finances
Sound Business Principles
Sound Investments
Surviving the 90's Economy
Wills and Trusts
Your Financial Future

Other Books:

The Coming Economic Earthquake
Debt-Free Living
The Financial Planning Workbook
How to Manage Your Money
Preparing for Retirement
Using Your Money Wisely
Your Finances in Changing Times

Videos:

The Financial Planning Workbook
How to Manage Your Money
Two Masters
Your Finances in Changing Times

Other Resources:

The Financial Planning Organizer
Debt-Free Living Cassette